2nd Grade Reading and Skills Practice with Favorite Bible Stories

Mighty Reader Workbook

Grade 2

written by
Heidi Cooley

B&H KIDS
EVERY little WORD MATTERS
BHKids.com

Dedication

For Jeff: My dear husband and biggest fan, thank you for believing in me and encouraging me to take on this project!

For Savannah and Shepard: Thank you for your patience and support during the writing process!

For my parents: Thank you for the endless examples of creativity, doing BIG things for the Lord, and having the courage to try new things in life.

For my students: Your hard work and dedication will take you on many reading adventures! Keep up the good work!

DEWEY: C372.4
SUBHD: READING \ READING READINESS \
BIBLE--STUDY AND TEACHING

Printed in Shenzhen, Guangdong, China in February 2018
1 2 3 4 5 6 • 22 21 20 19 18

Dear Parents,

During my thirteen years of teaching, I have learned the importance of daily reading and the impact it has on a child's learning development. Although your child reads a lot in the classroom, he or she needs an additional twenty minutes of reading at home as well. So it's crucial that you become a reading partner. Parents constantly ask me, "How can I help my child with reading? What should he be reading? What questions do I ask her after she has read?" These questions gave me the idea of using God's Word to practice the reading standards and skills your child learns in the classroom. It's a way of ending your child's day with reading practice *and* Bible learning!

In the *Mighty Reader Workbook*, I offer thirteen week-long lessons, each focusing on one story for six days. Your child will read the story in a different way each day and will be asked different questions. Be sure to refer to the Reading Strategies Guide on page 6 to understand how you will read with your child. The lessons will be similar throughout the book, which provides your child with the repetitive structure necessary for extra reading practice and gaining fluency.

Encourage your child to read aloud the questions to you. If he struggles, help him with the words. Also encourage him to look back in the text for answers, which is a skill he is learning in school. I've created questions for each lesson that align with the reading skills and standards taught in second grade. The questions include verbiage your child should be familiar with from his teacher. This workbook is not designed for your child to do alone. It is geared for parents as partners. Partner with your child to create a better reader!

As a parent, I know how difficult it can be to get homework completed each night and try to have a devotional time with your child too. My goal is to help your child complete the suggested twenty minutes of reading each night in God's Word and get skills practice too! I hope you enjoy the *Mighty Reader Workbook*!

Blessings,

Heidi Cooley

Contents

Old Testament Stories

New Testament Stories

Reading Strategies Guide

Every week, your child is introduced to a new Bible story to be read using a different strategy each day. This repetition helps increase reading fluency, the ability to read text smoothly and accurately.

- Echo Read. The adult reads one or two sentences aloud, and then the child repeats those same sentences. Encourage the reader to touch each word as he reads aloud.

- Choral Read. The adult and the child read the story at the same time. Encourage the child to track the words with her finger in a continuous motion as she reads along.

- Cloze Read. The adult begins reading the story aloud and pauses on a specific word in each sentence to allow the child to fill in the word that comes next.

- Partner Read. The adult reads a sentence or paragraph aloud, and then the child reads the next sentence or paragraph aloud. Encourage the child to track the words with her finger.

- Independent Read. The adult listens to the child read aloud the text independently. If a child gets stuck on a word, ask him to try to sound out the word. Give clues if necessary in order to move onto the next word.

- Fluency Check. The adult sets the timer for one minute and asks the child to read the passage as quickly as possible. Once the timer is done, the adult counts the words read correctly to see how many the child reads in one minute. (See "Reading Skills Guide" on the next page.)

Reading Skills Guide

- Key Details. This area assesses a child's comprehension of the passage by asking him to read and identify different key details such as main idea; character/setting; problem/solution; cause/effect; who, what, when, where, why, and how questions; and sequencing the events.

- Visualization. With this skill the child will create a picture in his mind to demonstrate comprehension. Drawing a picture is one way to practice and demonstrate understanding of the text.

- Text Features. This skill connects to non-fiction text. The student practices or locates items in the text such as labels, headings, bold print, and captions.

- Context Clues. With this skill the reader will determine the meaning of words and multiple-meaning words based on the context of the sentence or passage.

- Phonics. This skill allows students to work with words and their sounds.

- Connecting Writing with Reading. A writing component is connected to the passage each week. The child is asked to write a response to the passage. Encourage him to use correct punctuation and letter formation. Reading and writing go hand in hand, and both are necessary to become a strong reader.

- Fluency. Each lesson is designed to last around twenty minutes and have the child read each day. Repetition is one of the keys to increasing reading fluency and is practiced in the daily lessons. The goal for a second grader is to read 82 wpm (words per minute) on grade-level text by the end of second grade. To practice, set the timer and have your child read the passage for one minute. Count the words read correctly to get an idea of where your child's ability lies.

- Decoding. This skill asks the students to decode or sound out a word. It's critical that the reader know her letter sounds to be able to decode correctly.

God's 7-Day Masterpiece

Vocabulary

The list of words below will be in the story. Take a few minutes to discuss the meanings of these words with your child before beginning to read. Ask your child to repeat them to you and use them in a sentence.

existed: lived

separate: to move apart

divided: broken into parts

symbol: an object that stands for or represents something else

image: likeness, appearance

masterpiece: an amazing work of art

Biblical terms: God, Spirit of God

Skills

Refer to the Reading Skills Guide on page 7 for a detailed explanation about many of these skills.

Sequencing

Context Clues

Key Details

Visualization

Punctuation

Inferencing

Phonics

Connecting Writing with Reading

Determining the Lesson

Text Features

Vocabulary

God's 7-Day Masterpiece

Genesis 1:1–2:3

1. In the beginning, **God** was all that **existed**. Then He created the heavens and the earth. There was darkness all around. The **Spirit of God** quietly moved over the waters.

2. On the *first* day, God said, "Let there be light." He liked the light! He decided to **separate** the light from the darkness. He called the light day and the darkness night.

3. On the *second* day, God made the sky. On the *third* day, He **divided** the sky from the waters and caused dry ground to appear. He called the dry part land, and the waters He called seas. The land grew beautiful plants and trees. God liked this too!

4. On the *fourth* day, God created evening and morning. He used the sun as a **symbol** for day and the moon as a symbol for night. On the *fifth* day, He created birds for the sky and creatures for the sea. He liked the birds and sea creatures!

5. On the *sixth* day God made all kinds of animals for the land. He created livestock and wild animals. Then He made man and woman in His own **image**. God blessed them. He saw all that He had done was good!

6. God had completed His **masterpiece**. Then He used the *seventh* day to rest from His work. God is an amazing creator!

Don't ever forget God's power, Mighty Reader. You were made in His image too!

Day 1

Skills: Sequencing Events

1 Read the story as an *echo read* with someone in your home.

2 In the text, circle all the number words with (yellow). (Hint: There are seven.)

3 *Sequence* each day's events from the story, and fill in the chart below. Be sure to put them in order from beginning to end.

Which day?	What was created?

Day 2

Skills: Context Clues, Key Details

1 Read the story as a *choral read* with someone in your home.

2 Reread paragraph 1. How did the Spirit of God move over the waters? Write your answer in the box.

3 What is the root word in the word **quietly**? Write your answer in box 1. In the text, circle the word **quietly** in (blue). What do you think this word means? Write your answer in box 2.

1.
2.

4 Reread paragraph 2. What did God do with the light and darkness? Underline evidence in yellow. Write your answer in the box.

Day 3

Skills: Visualization, Context Clues, Punctuation

1 Read the story as a *cloze read* with someone in your home.

2 Reread paragraph 4. In box 1, draw a symbol of what God used for the light. In box 2, draw a symbol of what God used for the darkness. Underline evidence in the text in <u>orange</u>. Write the words under the pictures.

1.	2.

3 What does the word **symbol** mean?

○ An instrument
○ A feeling about something
○ An object or picture that represents something else

4 Use the word **symbol** in a sentence of your own. Write it in the box. Be sure to use correct punctuation.

Day 4

Skills: Key Details, Inferencing, Phonics

1. Read the story as a *partner read* with someone in your home.

2. Reread paragraph 5. Who did God create in His own **image**?
   Underline evidence in <u>blue</u>. Write your answer in the box.

3. Reread the story. How did God feel about His creation? Write your
   answer in the box.

4. Reread this sentence: *God had completed His* **masterpiece**. A
   masterpiece is an amazing work of art. Write the word **masterpiece**
   in the box. Trace the vowels in **yellow** and the consonants in **orange**.

Day 5

Skills: Connecting Writing with Reading, Determining the Lesson

1 Read the story as an *independent reader* to someone in your home. Ask for help if you get stuck on a word. You are a wonderful reader!

2 On the lines below, write answers to the following questions: *What is your favorite part about the creation story? Why is it your favorite?*

Use the guide below for writing your paragraph. Sentence 1 is your topic sentence. Sentences 2–4 support your topic sentence. Sentence 5 is your concluding sentence.

Topic Sentence: Write a sentence that begins with *"My favorite part of the creation story is . . ."*

_____ .

Supporting Sentence: *I like it because . . .*

_____ .

Supporting Sentence: *It's amazing because . . .*

_____ .

Supporting Sentence: *I'm thankful for it because . . .*

_____ .

Concluding Sentence: Think of a sentence to end your paragraph!

_____ .

After you finish your sentences, read them aloud to someone in your home.

Day 6

Skills: Visualization, Making Connections, Text Features

Reread paragraph 4. Use your writing tools to *draw and color a picture*. Illustrate what God created on the *fifth* day. After drawing your picture, write a *caption* under your illustration that talks about what God created on the *fifth* day.

Write your caption in the box below.

Fluency Check

Set the timer for one minute, and see how many words in the story you can read correctly. You are a Mighty Reader!

Adam and Eve

Vocabulary

The list of words below will be in the story. Take a few minutes to discuss the meanings of these words with your child before beginning to read. Ask your child to repeat them to you and use them in a sentence.

delicious: very tasty

knowledge: facts and information

crafty: dishonest, sly

forbidden: not allowed

convinced: persuaded, talked someone into something

blamed: found someone guilty

Biblical terms: God, Garden of Eden, Adam, the tree of the knowledge of good and evil, Eve

Skills

Refer to the Reading Skills Guide on page 7 for a detailed explanation about many of these skills.

Key Details	Determining the Lesson
Context Clues	Visualization
Inferencing	Text Features
Making Connections	Vocabulary
Connecting Writing with Reading	

Adam and Eve

Genesis 2:8–3:24

1. **God** created a place called the **Garden of Eden**. It was a place filled with beautiful trees and **delicious** fruit. God needed someone to work in the garden to take care of it. He chose the man He created. His name was **Adam**.

2. In the middle of the garden stood a tree known as **the tree of the knowledge of good and evil**. God told Adam that he could eat from any tree except for this one. God said Adam would die if he ate fruit from this tree.

3. God began to see that Adam was lonely. He felt it was not good for man to be alone. He needed a helper. While Adam was sleeping, God took one of his ribs. He used this rib to form a woman. Her name was **Eve**. Adam and Eve became man and wife.

4. One day a **crafty** serpent spoke to Eve. He told her she would be like God if she ate the fruit from the **forbidden** tree. The serpent said she would not die. He **convinced** her to eat a piece of the fruit. She decided to share some with Adam too.

5. After Adam and Eve ate the fruit, they felt afraid. They made clothes out of leaves and hid from God. God asked if they had eaten the fruit. Adam **blamed** Eve, and Eve blamed the serpent. God punished the serpent. He would forever crawl on his belly and eat dust.

6. God also punished Adam and Eve. They had to leave the garden forever. Before they left, God made clothes for them.

It is important to make good choices in your life. God will help you to obey, Mighty Reader!

Day 1:

Skills: Key Details

1 Read the story as an *echo read* with someone in your home.

2 Who are the main characters in this story? Write your answers in the boxes.

3 What is the *setting* of this story? In the text, circle the setting in (yellow) in paragraph 1. Write the setting in the box.

4 What is the *problem* in the story? Write your answer in the box.

5 How does God solve the *problem*? Write your answer in the box.

Day 2

Skills: Key Details

1 Read the story as a *choral read* with someone in your home.

2 Reread paragraph 2. What stood in the middle of the garden? Write your answer in the box.

```
[                                    ]
```

3 What did God say would happen if Adam ate fruit from the tree of the knowledge of good and evil? Underline evidence in the text in yellow. Write your answer in the box.

```
[                                    ]
```

4 Reread paragraph 3. Why did God think Adam needed a helper? Underline evidence in blue. Write your answer in the box.

```
[                                    ]
```

Day 3

Skills: Key Details, Context Clues

1 Read the story as a *cloze read* with someone in your home.

2 Reread paragraph 4. In the text, circle the word **crafty** in (orange). What do you think the word **crafty** means?

```



```

3 Draw a line and match the characters to their actions.

God	Took care of the garden
serpent	Gave Adam a helper
Eve	Convinced Eve to eat the fruit
Adam	Blamed the serpent

4 Reread this sentence: *The serpent convinced her to eat a piece of the fruit.* What do you think the word **convinced** means? Write your answer in the box.

```



```

Day 4

Skills: Inferencing, Making Connections

1. Read the story as a *partner read* with someone in your home.

2. Reread paragraph 4. How do you think Eve felt after she ate the forbidden fruit? Write your answer in the box.

   ┌───┐
   │   │
   │   │
   │   │
   │   │
   └───┘

3. Reread paragraph 5. Why do you think Adam and Eve blamed others instead of taking responsibility for their choices? Write your answer in the box.

   ┌───┐
   │   │
   │   │
   │   │
   │   │
   └───┘

4. Think about the story of Jonah and the big fish. (You can find the story in the book of Jonah in the Bible.) Make a connection between Jonah's actions and Adam and Eve's actions. How are they similar? Write your answer in the box.

   ┌───┐
   │   │
   │   │
   │   │
   └───┘

Day 5

Skills: Connecting Writing with Reading, Determining the Lesson

1 Read the story as an *independent reader* to someone in your home. Ask for help if you get stuck on a word. You are becoming an awesome reader!

2 On the lines below, write about the following: *The garden was filled with delicious fruit. What type of fruit would you have eaten in the Garden of Eden? Explain why.*

Use the guide below for writing your paragraph. Sentence 1 is your topic sentence. Sentences 2–4 support your topic sentence. Sentence 5 is your concluding sentence.

Topic Sentence: Write a sentence on the line that begins with *"The fruit I would have eaten in the garden would have been . . ."*

_____ .

Supporting Sentence: What does the fruit look like?

_____ .

Supporting Sentence: How does the fruit taste?

_____ .

Supporting Sentence: Why did you choose this fruit?

_____ .

Concluding Sentence: Think of a sentence to end your paragraph!

_____ .

After you finish your sentences, read them aloud to someone in your home.

Day 6

Skills: Visualization, Making Connections, Text Features

Use your writing tools to *draw and color a picture*. Draw a picture of what you think the *tree of the knowledge of good and evil* might have looked like. Be sure to place it in the middle of the garden. *Label* different parts of your tree with words such as *leaves, branches, fruit, trunk, grass,* and *sky.*

Practice reading your labels aloud to someone.

Fluency Check

Set the timer for one minute and see how many words in the story you can read correctly. You are a Mighty Reader!

A Story of Two Brothers

Vocabulary

The list of words below will be in the story. Take a few minutes to discuss the meanings of these words with your child before beginning to read. Ask your child to repeat them to you and use them in a sentence.

skillful: talented

favor: to prefer someone over someone else

stew: a slow-cooked dish of meat and vegetables

birthright: special privileges and inheritance belonging to the firstborn son

deceived: tricked

blessing: gifts and approval

Biblical terms: **Isaac, Rebekah, God, Esau, Jacob**

Skills

Refer to the Reading Skills Guide on page 7 for a detailed explanation about many of these skills.

Key Details

Compare/Contrast

Sequencing

Context Clues

Word Analysis

Inferencing

Determining the Lesson

Connecting Writing with Reading

Visualization

Sentences

Vocabulary

A Story of Two Brothers

Genesis 25:20–34; 27:1–45; 33:1–4

1. There was a man named **Isaac**. He married a woman named **Rebekah**. Isaac prayed to **God** that his wife could have a baby. God answered his prayer. God told Rebekah she was going to have twins!

2. Soon she had twin baby boys. The first baby was red and hairy. He was named **Esau**. The second baby came out grabbing his brother's heel. He was named **Jacob**.

3. Over time, the boys grew up. Esau loved to be outside. He became a **skillful** hunter. Isaac enjoyed this about his son. Jacob was just the opposite. He was a quiet man and chose to stay around the tents. Rebekah enjoyed this about her son. She began to **favor** Jacob.

4. One day, Jacob was near the tents cooking some **stew**. Esau had just come home from hunting. He was very hungry. Esau asked his brother for some stew. His brother made Esau promise to sell his **birthright** to Jacob. Esau was so hungry that he agreed.

5. As time passed, Jacob **deceived** his brother again. Their father, Isaac, became very old and couldn't see. Isaac wanted to give Esau his blessing. Rebekah convinced Jacob to dress up as Esau. Jacob wore his brother's clothes and put hairy goatskin on his arms. Jacob smelled and felt like Esau, so Isaac blessed him. That day, Jacob stole his brother's **blessing**.

6. Esau was very upset and hurt by his brother. He wanted the blessing! Many years later, Esau would forgive Jacob. They would be friends again.

Always tell the truth, Mighty Reader, and be kind to your brothers and sisters. This will please God!

Day 1

Skills: Key Details, Compare/Contrast

1 Read the story as an *echo read* with someone in your home.

2 Who are the brothers in this story? Write your answers in the boxes.

3 Think about Jacob and Esau. Let's compare and contrast these characters. Write your answers in the boxes.

How are they alike?

How are they different?

Jacob:	Esau:

Day 2

Skills: Key Details, Sequencing

1 Read the story as a *choral read* with someone in your home.

2 Reread paragraph 2. What was the main event that happened at the *beginning* of the story? Write your answer in the box.

3 Reread paragraph 4. What happened to Esau in the *middle* of the story? Underline evidence in yellow. Write your answer in the box.

4 Reread paragraph 5. What did Jacob take from his brother at the *end* of the story? Underline evidence in <u>blue</u>. Write your answer in the box.

5 In the text, circle the word **skillful** in (green). Use the word **skillful** in a sentence of your own. Write it on the line.

Day 3

Skills: Context Clues, Word Analysis, Key Details

1 Read the story as a *cloze read* with someone in your home.

2 Reread paragraph 3. Circle the word **favor** in (orange). What do you think the word **favor** means?

3 In the text, circle the word **birthright** in (red). This is a **compound word**. What two words are used in this compound word? Write them in the boxes.

4 In the text, circle the word **deceived** in (blue). What would be a *synonym*, a word that means the same thing, for **deceived**? Write your answer in the box.

5 What is the *setting* in paragraph 4? Write your answer in the box.

Day 4

Skills: Inferencing, Determining the Lesson

1 Read the story as a *partner read* with someone in your home.

2 Reread paragraph 5. How did Jacob trick his father and take Esau's blessing? Write your answer in the box.

3 After reading this story, what can you *infer*, or figure out, about what kind of person **Jacob** was? How would you describe him? Write your answer in the box.

4 After reading this story, what can you *infer*, or figure out, about what kind of person **Esau** was? How would you describe him? Write your answer in the box.

5 What is a *lesson* you can learn from this story? Write your answer in the box.

Day 5

Skills: Connecting Writing with Reading

1 Read the story as an *independent reader* to someone in your home. Ask for help if you get stuck on a word. Keep practicing; you can do it!

2 On the lines below, write about the following: *Esau was a skillful hunter. What are you skillful at doing?*

Use the guide below for writing your paragraph. Sentence 1 is your topic sentence. Sentences 2–4 support your topic sentence. Sentence 5 is your concluding sentence.

Topic Sentence: Write a sentence that begins with *"I am skillful at . . ."*

_____ .

Supporting Sentence: *I am skillful because . . .*

_____ .

Supporting Sentence: *I am also skillful because . . .*

_____ .

Supporting Sentence: *Another reason I am skillful is . . .*

_____ .

Concluding Sentence: Think of a sentence to end your paragraph!

_____ .

After you finish your sentences, read them aloud to someone in your home.

Day 6

Skills: Visualization, Key Details, Sentences

Use your writing tools to *draw and color a picture*. Use the two boxes below to draw a picture of Jacob and Esau. Use key details from the story to draw their pictures correctly. Write a sentence about Jacob and Esau below your pictures.

Jacob	Esau

Jacob: _____

Esau: _____

Fluency Check

Set the timer for one minute, and see how many words in the story you can read correctly. You are a Mighty Reader!

A Baby in a Basket

Vocabulary

The list of words below will be in the story. Take a few minutes to discuss the meanings of these words with your child before beginning to read. Ask your child to repeat them to you and use them in a sentence.

grow: to gain more of something

protect: to keep safe

tar: a dark, thick liquid used for waterproofing

reeds: tall, slender plants that grow in the water

compassion: concern for others

real: true or actual

leader: a person who leads or commands

Biblical terms: **Pharaoh, Egypt, Hebrew, Nile River, Pharaoh's daughter, Moses, God**

Skills

Refer to the Reading Skills Guide on page 7 for a detailed explanation about many of these skills.

Key Details	Determining the Lesson
Inferencing	Visualization
Sequencing	Text Features
Context Clues	Vocabulary
Connecting Writing with Reading	

A Baby in a Basket

Exodus 1:8–2:10

1. A ruler named **Pharaoh** lived in **Egypt**. He was very powerful. He ruled over the **Hebrew** people. The Hebrews continued to **grow** in number. He worried that they would someday fight against him.

2. Pharaoh did something terrible. He got rid of all the Hebrew baby boys. But there was one baby who got away. His mother began to worry about his safety. She could no longer hide him. She came up with a plan to **protect** her baby.

3. His mother took a basket. She covered it with **tar**. This would keep the water out and the baby dry. She placed her baby in the basket. Then she put it in the **Nile River** near the **reeds**. The basket began to float.

4. Out in the river was the **Pharaoh's daughter**. She saw the basket. She asked her helper to bring it to her. She saw a baby, and it was crying. She had **compassion** for the baby. She found it was a Hebrew and knew it was in danger.

5. Pharaoh's daughter chose to help the baby. She paid a Hebrew woman to nurse and care for it. It was actually the baby's **real** mother! As the baby grew up, Pharaoh's daughter raised the baby as her son. She named him **Moses**.

6. Moses would grow up to be a great **leader** of the Hebrew people. **God** would use him in many ways. God was with Moses.

God will always be with you too, Mighty Reader!

Day 1

1. Read the story as an *echo read* with someone in your home.

2. How did Moses' mother react to the *problem* in the story? Write your answer in the boxes.

3. Reread paragraph 2. Why do you think Moses' mother could no longer keep her baby safe? Write your answer in the box.

4. How did Moses' mother make the basket safe? Write your answer in the box.

5. How did the tar help the basket? Write your answer in the box.

Day 2

Skills: Key Details

1 Read the story as a *choral read* with someone in your home.

2 Reread paragraph 1. Who was the leader of Egypt? Circle his name in (blue). Write your answer in the box.

```



```

3 Why was the leader worried about the Hebrew people? Underline evidence in yellow. Write your answer in the box.

```



```

4 Reread paragraph 2. What did Pharaoh decide to do about the Hebrew babies? Underline evidence in green. Write your answer in the box.

```



```

Day 3

Skills: Inferencing, Sequencing, Context Clues

1. Read the story as a *cloze read* with someone in your home.

2. Reread paragraphs 4 and 5. How would you describe the Pharaoh's daughter based on her actions in the story?

3. Number the events below in the order they appear in paragraphs 4 and 5.

	She saw a basket with a baby.
	Pharaoh's daughter raised the baby as her son.
	She chose to help the baby.
	Out in the river was the Pharaoh's daughter.

4. Reread this sentence: *She had compassion for the baby.* What do you think the word compassion means? Write your answer in the box.

Day 4

Skills: Inferencing, Key Details

1 Read the story as a *partner read* with someone in your home.

2 Reread paragraph 1. What does it mean when the text says **"the Hebrew people continued to grow in number"**? Write your answer in the box.

[ ]

3 Reread paragraph 5. Why do you think the Pharaoh's daughter chose a Hebrew woman to care for the baby? Write your answer in the box.

[ ]

4 Which Hebrew woman did she end up choosing? Write your answer in box 1. What does this tell you about God? Write your answer in box 2.

1.

2.

Day 5

Skills: Connecting Writing with Reading, Determining the Lesson

1 Read the story as an *independent reader* to someone in your home. Ask for help if you get stuck on a word. Keep practicing, and you will become a stronger reader!

2 On the lines below, write about the following: *Moses' mother showed courage in this story. How did his mother show courage?*

Use the guide below for writing your paragraph. Sentence 1 is your topic sentence. Sentences 2–4 support your topic sentence. Sentence 5 is your concluding sentence.

Topic Sentence: Copy this sentence on the line below: *Moses' mother showed courage in many ways.*

_____ .

Supporting Sentence: What did she make for the baby?

_____ .

Supporting Sentence: What did she do with the baby?

_____ .

Supporting Sentence: How did she help the baby?

_____ .

Concluding Sentence: Think of a sentence to end your paragraph!

_____ .

After you finish your sentences, read them aloud to someone in your home.

Day 6

Skills: Visualization, Text Features

Use your writing tools to *draw and color a picture.* Draw a picture of baby Moses in a basket floating down the Nile River. *Label* different parts of your picture with words such as *Moses, basket, tar, Nile River, riverbank, grass,* and *sky.*

Practice reading your labels aloud to someone.

Fluency Check

Set the timer for one minute, and see how many words in the story you can read correctly. You are a Mighty Reader!

A Bush and a Fire

Vocabulary

The list of words below will be in the story. Take a few minutes to discuss the meanings of these words with your child before beginning to read. Ask your child to repeat them to you and use them in a sentence.

slaves: people who were owned by others and worked very hard without pay

treated: dealt with in a certain way

flame: a sheet of fire

shocked: surprised

miserable: unhappy and uncomfortable

confident: feeling certain that you can do something

Biblical terms: **God, Hebrew, Moses, Egypt, angel, holy ground**

Skills

Refer to the Reading Skills Guide on page 7 for a detailed explanation about many of these skills.

Character's Point of View

Key Details

Understanding Words and Phrases

Word Analysis

Phonics

Connecting Writing with Reading

Main Idea

Visualization

Text Features

Vocabulary

A Bush and a Fire

Exodus 3:1–12

1 **God** wanted to help the **Hebrew** people. They were still **slaves** in Egypt. They cried out for help, and He heard their cries. God would use a man to help the people. His name was **Moses**.

2 At this time, Moses no longer lived in **Egypt**. He did not like how the pharaoh **treated** the Hebrew slaves. Moses was now married and had become a shepherd. One day he visited a mountainside on the far side of the desert.

3 On the mountainside, the **angel** of the Lord appeared to him. It was in the form of a **flame** of fire inside of a bush! Moses was **shocked**! Even though the bush was on fire, it did not burn up. He decided to get a closer look.

4 As he came upon the bush, he heard a voice. God said, "Moses! Moses!" Then Moses replied, "Here I am." God told him to take off his sandals. He was standing on **holy ground**. God said He was the God of Moses' father. This made Moses feel afraid, so he hid his face.

5 God said the Hebrew people were **miserable**. He told Moses that He had chosen Moses to help the people. God said He wanted Moses to bring His people out of Egypt. Moses felt afraid. He wasn't **confident** he could do the job very well. God said, "I will be with you." After talking to God, Moses obeyed.

6 God gave Moses all he needed to help free the Hebrew people.

> **When something seems hard, ask God for help, Mighty Reader!**

Day 1

Skills: Character's Point of View

1 Read the story as an *echo read* with someone in your home.

2 Let's think about a *character's point of view*—how he thinks and feels about something. What was Moses' *point of view* about going to Egypt when God first asked him to do the job? How did he think and feel about the job? Write your answer on the lines in the box.

3 How did Moses' *point of view* change after he talked with God for a while? Write your answer on the lines in the box.

Day 2

Skills: Key Details

1 Read the story as a *choral read* with someone in your home.

2 Reread paragraph 3. What is the *setting* of this paragraph? Circle the setting in (blue). Write your answer in the box.

```

```

3 What did Moses see in the bush? Write your answer in box 1. What did the angel look like? Write your answer in box 2.

1.
2.

4 Why was Moses shocked by what he saw? Underline evidence in yellow. Write your answer in the box.

```

```

Day 3

Skills: Key Details: Understanding Words and Phrases

1. Read the story as a *cloze read* with someone in your home.

2. Reread paragraph 1. What does the text mean when it says, **"they cried out for help"**? Write your answer in the box.

3. Reread paragraph 3. What does the text mean when it says, **"to get a closer look"**? Write your answer in the box.

4. Reread paragraph 4. Why do you think Moses **"hid his face"**? Write your answer in the box.

5. Reread paragraph 5. What does the text mean when it says, **"bring His people out of Egypt"**? Write your answer in the box.

Day 4

Skills: Word Analysis, Phonics

1   Read the story as a *partner read* with someone in your home.

2   Find the word **mountainside** in the text, and circle it in (orange). This
    is a *compound word*. What two words form the word **mountainside**?
    Write them in the boxes.

3   Find the word **flame** in the text, and circle it in (red). Think of a word
    that *rhymes* with **flame**. Write it in the box.

| |
| |
| |

4   Find the word **miserable** in the text, and circle it in (green). Write
    the word **miserable** in the box. Trace the *vowels* in orange and the
    consonants in yellow.

| |
| |
| |

5   Find the word **confident** in the text, and circle it in (purple). How
    many *syllables* are in the word **confident**? You can clap out the word
    to help you. Write your answer in the box.

| |
| |
| |

Day 5

Skills: Connecting Writing with Reading, Main Idea

1 Read the story as an *independent reader* to someone in your home. Ask for help if you get stuck on a word. You are a wonderful reader!

2 On the lines below, write about the following question: *How does God show His power in this story?*

Use the guide below for writing your paragraph. Sentence 1 is your topic sentence. Sentences 2–4 support your topic sentence. Sentence 5 is your concluding sentence.

Topic Sentence: Copy this sentence on the line below: *God shows His power to Moses.*

_____ .

Supporting Sentence: How does the angel appear?

_____ .

Supporting Sentence: Why is the fire amazing?

_____ .

Supporting Sentence: How does God speak to Moses?

_____ .

Concluding Sentence: Think of a sentence to end your paragraph!

_____ .

After you finish your sentences, read them aloud to someone in your home.

Day 6

Skills: Visualization, Text Features

Reread paragraph 4. Use your writing tools to *draw and color a picture.* Illustrate the burning bush on the mountainside. After drawing your picture, write a *heading* above your illustration that talks about the burning bush. A heading usually appears at the top of a page and gives information about the text or a picture. It often appears in **bold print.**

Heading

Fluency Check

Set the timer for one minute, and see how many words in the story you can read correctly. You are a Mighty Reader!

Joshua and the Walls

Vocabulary

The list of words below will be in the story. Take a few minutes to discuss the meanings of these words with your child before beginning to read. Ask your child to repeat them to you and use them in a sentence.

journey: a long trip

promised: did what one said one would do

spies: people who secretly watch and collect information

priests: men in the Bible who were descendants of Aaron, Moses' brother

trumpet: a musical instrument

spared: let go, saved

destroyed: ruined

Biblical terms: **Moses, Hebrew, Promised Land, God, Joshua, Jordan River, Jericho, Rahab, Ark of the Covenant**

Skills

Refer to the Reading Skills Guide on page 7 for a detailed explanation about many of these skills.

Key Details	Determining the Lesson
Sequencing	Connecting Writing with Reading
Context Clues	Visualization
Word Analysis	Text Features
Problem/Solution	Vocabulary

Joshua and the Walls

Joshua 1:1–5; 2:1–4; 6:1–27

1. With **Moses** as their leader, the **Hebrew** people were no longer slaves. They were on a **journey** to the **Promised Land**. After Moses died, **God** chose another leader for the people. His name was **Joshua**.

2. Joshua led his people to the **Jordan River**. On the other side of the river was the city of **Jericho**. This was the land God had **promised** the Hebrew people. All they had to do was take over the land. So Joshua sent two **spies** to the city. A woman named **Rahab** helped his spies. She hid the men inside the city walls. Then they could spy on the land.

3. A huge wall went around the city. The people of Jericho knew the Hebrews were close by. So they locked their gates. God told Joshua that Jericho would be his. However, he would need to follow His plan.

4. God told Joshua to walk around the walls of the city one time each day. They had to do this for six days. Some **priests** had to carry the **Ark of the Covenant**. On the seventh day, the people had to march around the city seven times. Then seven other priests had to blow their **trumpets**. The rest of the people had to shout. Then God would give them their city.

5. Joshua and his people followed God's plan. The walls crashed down! The Hebrews took over the land! Rahab and her family were **spared** because she had helped the spies. Everything else was **destroyed**.

6. God kept His promise. He gave the city of Jericho to the Hebrews. God helped the people win the battle. He took care of their needs.

You can always trust God, Mighty Reader!

49

Day 1

Skills: Key Details

1 Read the story as an *echo read* with someone in your home.

2 *Who* did God choose as the new leader of the Hebrew people? In the text, circle his name in (blue). Write your answer in the box.

3 Reread paragraph 2. *Where* did Joshua lead his people? Underline evidence in yellow. Write your answer in the box.

4 *What* did Joshua do to get a better look at the city of Jericho? Underline evidence in green. Write your answer in the box.

Day 2

Skills: Sequencing

1 Read the story as a *choral read* with someone in your home.

2 Reread paragraph 4. Use the word bank to *sequence* the events of this part of the story.

Word Bank

trumpets   shout   seven   walls   give   priests   six

God told Joshua to walk around the _____ of the city one time each day.

They had to do this for _____ days.

Some _____ had to carry the **Ark of the Covenant**.

On the seventh day, the people had to march around the city _____ times.

Then seven other priests had to blow their _____.

The rest of the people had to _____.

Then God would _____ them their city.

3 How do you think Joshua felt after he heard God's plan?

_____

Day 3

Skills: Context Clues, Word Analysis

1 Read the story as a *cloze read* with someone in your home.

2 In the text, circle the word spared in (orange). What do you think the word spared means?

3 In the text, circle the word spies in (red). What is a word that *rhymes* with spies? Write it in the box.

4 In the text, circle the word journey in (blue). What would be a *synonym*, a word that means the same thing, for journey? Write your answer in the box.

5 In the text, circle the word promised in (yellow). Write the word promised in the box. Trace the *vowels* in yellow and the *consonants* in orange.

Day 4

Skills: Problem/Solution, Determining the Lesson

1 Read the story as a *partner read* with someone in your home.

2 Let's think about the *problem* and *solution* of this story. Fill in the graphic organizer below. Be sure to look back to the text to help you find your answers.

Problem	**Solution**
(Look in paragraph 3)	(Look in paragraph 5)

3 What is a *lesson* you can learn from this story? Write your answer on the lines in the box.

Day 5
Skills: Connecting Writing with Reading

1. Read the story as an *independent reader* to someone in your home. Ask for help if you get stuck on a word. Keep practicing; you can do it!

2. On the lines below, write about the following: *God keeps His promises. Make connections with two different stories about how God kept His promises. Think about Joshua in this story, and think about the story of Noah and the flood from Genesis in the Bible.*

Use the guide below for writing. Sentence 1 is your topic sentence. Sentences 2–4 support your topic sentence. Sentence 5 is your concluding sentence.

Topic Sentence: Copy this sentence on the line below: *God always keeps His promises.*

_____ .

Supporting Sentence: How did God keep His promise to the Hebrew people in this story?

_____ .

Supporting Sentence: What promise did God make after He flooded the earth in the story of Noah?

_____ .

Supporting Sentence: How has God kept the promise He made to Noah?

_____ .

Concluding Sentence: Think of a sentence to end your paragraph!

_____ .

After you finish your sentences, read them aloud to someone in your home.

Day 6

Use your writing tools to *draw and color a picture*. Draw a picture of the walls of Jericho. Draw some people marching around the walls. Draw the priests with their trumpets. *Label* different parts of your drawing. You can include labels such as *Jericho, walls, people, priests, Joshua, trumpets, sky,* and *grass.*

When you are finished, read your labels aloud to someone.

Fluency Check

Set the timer for one minute, and see how many words in the story you can read correctly. You are a Mighty Reader!

A Strong Man

Vocabulary

The list of words below will be in the story. Take a few minutes to discuss the meanings of these words with your child before beginning to read. Ask your child to repeat them to you and use them in a sentence.

strength: physical ability and power

secret: something that can't be shared with others

bothering: annoying someone or being a pest

blinded: when someone can no longer see

pillars: tall posts used to provide strength to a building

temple: a place of worship

Biblical terms: **Israelites, Philistines, God, Manoah, angel, Samson, Delilah**

Skills

Refer to the Reading Skills Guide on page 7 for a detailed explanation about many of these skills.

Key Details	Connecting Writing with Reading
Sequencing	Visualization
Inferencing	Text Features
Context Clues	Vocabulary

A Strong Man

Judges 13:1–7, 24; 15:14; 16:4–30

1. As time passed, the Israelites were making evil choices. They would not obey God. This made God upset. He decided to hand them over to the Philistines for forty years! The Philistines were mean and powerful.

2. Manoah and his wife obeyed God. His wife could not have a baby. One day an angel visited her. The angel said she would have a son. Her son would help save their people from the Philistines. To show he was obeying God, the boy should never cut his hair. Then God would give him great strength.

3. Manoah's wife soon gave birth. She named her boy Samson. He grew up, and God blessed him. He fell in love with a woman named Delilah. The Philistine leaders promised her a lot of money. She had to find the secret to Samson's strength.

4. Delilah worked very hard at finding out Samson's secret. She often asked him, "What makes you so strong?" She kept bothering him about his secret. Finally, he told her that his strength came from not cutting his long hair.

5. Delilah told the secret to the Philistine leaders. One day while Samson slept, they cut his hair. When he woke up, all his strength was gone. The Philistines blinded Samson and put him in prison.

6. God gave Samson strength one more time before he died. He stood between two pillars in their temple. He pushed the pillars with all his might. The temple crumbled to the ground on top of Samson and the Philistines. God used Samson to help save the Israelites.

God will give you strength too, Mighty Reader!

Day 1

1 Read the story as an *echo read* with someone in your home.

2 Fill in the chart below to name key details about the story of Samson.

Who is this story about?
What happens to Samson's hair?
When does Samson get his haircut?
Where is Samson when he pushes the pillars?
Why does Delilah want Samson to tell his secret?
How does Samson defeat the Philistines at the end of the story?

Day 2

Skills: Key Details

1. Read the story as a *choral read* with someone in your home.

2. Reread paragraph 1. Why did God hand over the Israelites to the Philistines? Underline evidence in <u>blue</u>. Write your answer in the box.

┌───┐
│   │
│   │
│   │
│   │
│   │
└───┘

3. Reread paragraph 2. Who obeyed God when others did not? Underline evidence in <u>yellow</u>. Write your answer in the box.

┌───┐
│   │
│   │
│   │
│   │
│   │
└───┘

4. After reading paragraph 2, answer this question: What message did the angel give to Manoah's wife? Underline evidence in <u>green</u>. Write your answer in the box.

┌───┐
│   │
│   │
│   │
│   │
└───┘

Day 3

Skills: Key Details, Sequencing

1 Read the story as a *cloze read* with someone in your home.

2 Reread paragraph 4. Where does Delilah think Samson's strength comes from? Write your answer in the box.

3 Reread paragraph 6. Where does Samson's strength really come from? Write your answer in the box.

4 Number the events in order as they appear in paragraphs 3–5.

	The Philistines cut Samson's hair.
	Samson falls in love with Delilah.
	Samson tells Delilah his secret.
	Delilah tells the Philistines Samson's secret.

Day 4

Skills: Inferencing, Context Clues

1 Read the story as a *partner read* with someone in your home.

2 Reread paragraph 1. What does it mean when the text says, **"He decided to hand them over to the Philistines"**? Write your answer in the box.

```

```

3 Reread paragraph 4. In the text, circle the word bothering in blue. What do you think the word bothering means? Write your answer in the box.

```

```

4 Reread paragraph 5. Why do you think the Philistines chose to cut Samson's hair while he was sleeping? Write your answer in the box.

```

```

5 In the text, circle the word pillars in paragraph 6. These were tall posts that helped to support the temple. Where else have you seen pillars? Write your answer in the box.

```

```

Day 5

Skills: Connecting Writing with Reading

1 Read the story as an *independent reader* to someone in your home. Ask for help if you get stuck on a word. Keep trying; you're doing great!

2 On the lines below, write about the following question: *Why was Samson special?*

Use the guide below for writing. Sentence 1 is your topic sentence. Sentences 2–4 support your topic sentence. Sentence 5 is your concluding sentence.

Topic Sentence: Copy this sentence on the line below: *Samson was a special man.*

_____ .

Supporting Sentence: What was special about the beginning of this story?

_____ .

Supporting Sentence: What was special about Samson's hair?

_____ .

Supporting Sentence: What was special about the ending of this story?

_____ .

Concluding Sentence: Think of a sentence to end your paragraph!

_____ .

After you finish your sentences, read them aloud to someone in your home.

Day 6

Skills: Visualization, Text Features

1 Use your writing tools to *draw and color a picture*. Draw a picture of Samson with his long hair. Write a *caption* at the bottom of your picture explaining how Samson's long hair helped him.

Caption

Practice reading your caption aloud to someone.

Fluency Check

Set the timer for one minute, and see how many words in the story you can read correctly. You are a Mighty Reader!

Fishers of Men

Vocabulary

The list of words below will be in the story. Take a few minutes to discuss the meanings of these words with your child before beginning to read. Ask your child to repeat them to you and use them in a sentence.

noticed: gave attention to

fishermen: men who fish

lower: to bring something down

agreed: felt the same about something

raise: to bring something up

amazed: shocked, surprised

followed: agreed with someone's views and went the same way

Biblical terms: **Jesus, Simon, James, John**

Skills

Refer to the Reading Skills Guide on page 7 for a detailed explanation about many of these skills.

Message of the Story	Connecting Writing with Reading
Context Clues	Problem/Solution
Key Details	Visualization
Text Features	Vocabulary
Word Analysis	

Fishers of Men

Luke 5:1–11

1 **Jesus** liked to talk to people about God. One day He talked to a crowd near a lake. He **noticed** two boats near the shore. He found that some **fishermen** owned the boats. Their names were **Simon**, **James**, and **John**.

2 Jesus walked over to the fishermen. They were busy washing their smelly nets. Jesus wanted to use one of their boats to teach the crowd. Jesus got on Simon's boat. Then Jesus taught the people from the boat.

3 Jesus finished His teaching. Then He told Simon to **lower** the nets into the deep water. Simon told Jesus that the fishermen had tried to catch fish all night. They had caught nothing. He still **agreed** to do as Jesus asked.

4 When the men lowered their nets, they were bursting with fish! There were so many fish that the nets began to rip! The fishermen had to call for help to **raise** their heavy nets. All the fish were causing the boat to sink! James and John ended up filling another boat with fish too.

5 Simon was **amazed** by this miracle! He fell to Jesus' feet. James and John were amazed too. Jesus told them not to be afraid. He told them they would become fishers of men now.

6 The fishermen sailed their boats to the land. They left everything and **followed** Jesus. They were some of His first disciples.

You can be a follower of Jesus and a fisher of men too. Share the love of Jesus with others, Mighty Reader!

Day 1

Skills: Message of the Story, Context Clues

1 Read the story as an *echo read* with someone in your home.

2 Let's think about the *message* in this story. Reread this sentence: *He told them they would become fishers of men now.* What is the *message* you can learn from this sentence? Write your answer on the lines in the box.

3 What does the word **followed** mean in this sentence? *They left everything and followed Jesus.* Write your answer on the lines in the box.

Day 2

Skills: Key Details

1. Read the story as a *choral read* with someone in your home.

2. Let's review the story's events. Write a sentence in each box that tells about what happened at the *beginning*, *middle*, and *end* of the story.

Beginning: (Paragraphs 1 and 2)

Middle: (Paragraphs 3 and 4)

End: (Paragraphs 5 and 6)

Day 3

Skills: Text Features, Word Analysis

1. Read the story as a *cloze read* with someone in your home.

2. Practice reading each of the vocabulary words below. These words are written in bold print in the story. This is a *text feature* that shows you that the word is important. Practice rewriting each of the words neatly in the boxes. Next, trace the *vowels* in yellow and count how many are in each word. Write your answers in the chart below.

Vocabulary Word	Rewrite the Word	Vowels
noticed		
fishermen		
lower		
agreed		
raise		
amazed		
followed		

Day 4

Skills: Key Details

1 Read the story as a *partner read* with someone in your home.

2 Reread paragraph 2. What were the fishermen doing when Jesus walked over? Underline evidence in yellow. Write your answer in the box.

3 Reread paragraph 4. What happened to the nets when the fishermen lowered them into the deep water? Underline evidence in red. Write your answer in the box.

4 Reread paragraph 5. What did Simon do after he saw the miracle? Underline evidence in green. Write your answer in the box.

Day 5

Skills: Connecting Writing with Reading, Problem/Solution

1 Read the story as an *independent reader* to someone in your home. Ask for help if you get stuck on a word. You're reading wonderfully! Keep up the good work!

2 Let's think about the problem and solution of this story. Follow the prompts below.

What was the *problem* the fishermen were having?

_____ .

How did they try to solve the *problem* at first?

_____ .

How did Jesus provide a *solution* in this story?

_____ .

How did the fishermen feel after Jesus provided a *solution*?

_____ .

What did the fishermen decide to do after the *solution*?

_____ .

After you finish your sentences, read them aloud to someone in your home.

Day 6

Use your writing tools to *draw and color a picture.* Draw a picture of the fishermen's nets bursting with fish. After drawing your picture, write a *caption* below your illustration that talks about the nets. You can look back in the story for key details. A *caption* is a sentence that gives a reader information about an illustration or photograph.

Caption

Fluency Check

Set the timer for one minute, and see how many words in the story you can read correctly. You are a Mighty Reader!

Jesus Heals Ten Men

Vocabulary

The list of words below will be in the story. Take a few minutes to discuss the meanings of these words with your child before beginning to read. Ask your child to repeat them to you and use them in a sentence.

leprosy: a skin disease

severe: serious, dreadful

contagious: spreading from one person to another

mercy: compassion

healed: made well again

faith: complete trust in someone

cure: a treatment that takes away a disease

Biblical terms: **Jesus, Jerusalem, Samaria, Galilee**

Skills

Refer to the Reading Skills Guide on page 7 for a detailed explanation about many of these skills.

Key Details	Inferencing
Compare/Contrast	Connecting Writing with Reading
Determining the Lesson	Visualization
Context Clues	Vocabulary

Jesus Heals Ten Men

Luke 17:11–19

1 **Jesus** was busy teaching and healing. One day He was on His way to a place called **Jerusalem**. He decided to pass through a village between **Samaria** and **Galilee**. Jesus soon met ten men. These men were very sick. They had **leprosy**. Leprosy was a **severe** skin disease. It was **contagious** and very painful!

2 The ten men stood away from Jesus because they were contagious. They began to shout. They asked Jesus to show them **mercy** and to heal them. Then Jesus told them to go visit the priest. While the men walked to the priest, they were **healed**!

3 One of the men noticed his body was healed. He was a **Samaritan**. He was not from the village. He quickly ran back to Jesus. He shouted, "Glory to God!" He fell to Jesus' feet and thanked Him!

4 Jesus asked about the other nine men. He reminded the man that He had healed ten men. Jesus was surprised that only the Samaritan returned to say thank you. He wasn't even from the village.

5 The Samaritan was thankful to be healed. Jesus told him to rise up. He told the man to continue on his way. His strong **faith** had healed him! So the thankful man left.

6 Jesus is a healer! He healed ten men with leprosy. It was a disease that didn't have a **cure**. Jesus was the cure! Only one came back to say thank you. It is important to say thank you. Jesus wants us to be thankful for the good things He has given us.

thank you!

Mighty Reader, remember to say thank you like the leper!

73

Day 1

Skills: Key Details

1 Read the story as an *echo read* with someone in your home.

2 Who are the *main characters* in this story? Write your answers in the box.

3 Reread paragraph 1. What is the *setting* of this story? Write your answer in the box.

4 Reread paragraph 2. What is the *problem* in the story? Write your answer in the box.

5 What was the *solution*? Write your answer in the box.

Day 2

Skills: Compare/Contrast, Determining the Lesson

1. Read the story as a *choral read* with someone in your home.

2. Let's compare and contrast the Samaritan from the other nine lepers.

How were the Samaritan and the other nine lepers alike?

How were they different?

Samaritan	Other Nine Lepers

3. What *lesson* can you learn from this story? Write your answer in the box.

Day 3

Skills: Key Details, Context Clues

1. Read the story as a *cloze read* with someone in your home.

2. Reread paragraph 1. In the text, circle the word **leprosy** in (orange).
   What does the word **leprosy** mean?

   [box]

3. Reread paragraph 2. Why did the ten men stand back from Jesus?
   Underline evidence in yellow. Write your answer in the box.

   [box]

4. Reread this sentence: *While the men walked to the priest, they were healed!* What do you think the word **healed** means? Write your answer in the box.

   [box]

Day 4

Skills: Inferencing, Key Details

1. Read the story as a *partner read* with someone in your home.

2. Reread paragraph 3. How do you think Jesus felt when the Samaritan came back to thank Him? Write your answer in the box.

3. Reread paragraph 5. What healed the Samaritan? Underline evidence in yellow. Write your answer in the box.

4. Reread paragraph 6. What does it mean when the text says, "**Jesus was the cure**"? Write your answer in the box.

Day 5

Skills: Connecting Writing with Reading

1 Read the story as an *independent reader* to someone in your home. Ask for help if you get stuck on a word. You are becoming an awesome reader!

2 On the lines below, write about the following: *This is a story about being thankful. Write about some things you are thankful for.*

Use the guide below for writing. Sentence 1 is your topic sentence. Sentences 2–4 support your topic sentence. Sentence 5 is your concluding sentence.

Topic Sentence: Copy this sentence on the line below: *I am thankful to God for many things.*

_____ .

Supporting Sentence: I am thankful for . . .

_____ .

Supporting Sentence: I am thankful for . . .

_____ .

Supporting Sentence: I am also thankful for . . .

_____ .

Concluding Sentence: Think of a sentence to end your paragraph!

_____ .

After you finish your sentences, read them aloud to someone in your home.

Day 6

Skills: Visualization, Key Details

Use your writing tools to *draw and color a picture*. Draw a picture of the Samaritan with leprosy in the first box. Draw a picture of the Samaritan after Jesus cured his leprosy in the second box.

With Leprosy	**Without Leprosy**

How did the Samaritan feel at the *beginning* of the story?

_____

How did the Samaritan feel at the *end* of the story?

_____

Fluency Check

Set the timer for one minute, and see how many words in the story you can read correctly. You are a Mighty Reader!

The Parable of Two Houses

Vocabulary

The list of words below will be in the story. Take a few minutes to discuss the meanings of these words with your child before beginning to read. Ask your child to repeat them to you and use them in a sentence.

parables: stories told to teach a spiritual lesson

wise: having knowledge and good judgment

firm: solid and strong

foundation: the surface on which a house is built

foolish: not having good judgment

weak: breakable, fragile

Biblical term: **Jesus**

Skills

Refer to the Reading Skills Guide on page 7 for a detailed explanation about many of these skills.

Key Details	Compare/Contrast
Story Events	Connecting Writing with Reading
Lesson	Visualization
Context Clues	Sentences
Word Analysis	Vocabulary

The Parable of Two Houses

Matthew 7:24–27

1 Do you like to listen to stories? When **Jesus** talked to the people, He told them great stories! These stories were called **parables**. The parables were used to teach the people lessons. They helped the people understand the ways of Jesus. The parables helped them to be more like Him.

2 One day Jesus told a parable about two different houses. The man who built the first house was **wise**. He took his time and built his house on a strong rock. When the rains, storms, and winds came, his house stood **firm**. The rock gave his house a strong **foundation**.

3 The man who built the second house was **foolish**. He rushed and built his house on soft sand. When the rains, storms, and winds came, his house fell apart. The soft sand gave his house a **weak** foundation.

4 Jesus used this parable to teach the people about strong foundations. Jesus said His words were like the rock. If the people obeyed and followed His words, their lives would have strong foundations. People would trust Jesus when bad things happened. They would be like the house built on the rock.

5 Jesus said those who did not listen to His words were like the foolish man. They would worry and be afraid when bad things happened to them. Their lives would not have a strong foundation. They would be like the house built on a weak pile of soft sand.

6 Think about a rock and a pile of sand. Which is stronger? Jesus wants us to trust in Him. He wants to be our strong foundation. This parable teaches us to read our Bible and follow the words of Jesus. Jesus is the Rock.

Choose to build your house on the Rock, Mighty Reader!

Day 1

Skills: Key Details

1　Read the story as an *echo read* with someone in your home.

2　Reread paragraph 1. *Who* told parables? Circle His name in (blue). Write your answer in the box.

3　Reread paragraph 2. *Where* did the wise man build his house? Underline evidence in yellow. Write your answer in the box.

4　Reread paragraph 3. *What* happened to the foolish man's house? Underline evidence in green. Write your answer in the box.

Day 2

Skills: Story Events, Lesson

1 Read the story as a *choral read* with someone in your home.

2 Reread paragraph 6. Use the word bank to retell the events of this part of the story.

Word Bank

Jesus   trust   foundation   build   parable   sand   stronger

Think about a rock and a pile of _____.

Which is _____?

Jesus wants us to _____in Him.

He wants to be our strong _____.

This _____ teaches us to read our Bible and follow the words of Jesus.

_____ is the Rock!

Choose to _____ your house on the Rock, Mighty Reader!

3 What is the *lesson* of this story?

_____

_____

Day 3

Skills: Context Clues, Word Analysis

1 Read the story as a *cloze read* with someone in your home.

2 In the text, circle the word **parables** in (orange). What are **parables**? Write your answer in the box.

```



```

3 In the text, circle the word **weak** in (red). What is a word that *rhymes* with **weak**? Write it in the box.

```



```

4 In the text, circle the word **wise** in (purple). What would be a *synonym*, a word that means the same thing, for **wise**? Write your answer in the box.

```



```

5 In the text, circle the word **foundation** in (yellow). Write the word **foundation** in the box. Trace the *vowels* in yellow and the *consonants* in orange.

```



```

Day 4

Skills: Compare/Contrast

1 Read the story as a *partner read* with someone in your home.

2 Let's *contrast* the foolish man with the wise man. List some things from the story that describe how they built their houses *differently*. Fill in the graphic organizer below. Be sure to look back in the text to help you find your answers.

Wise Man	Foolish Man
(Look in paragraph 2)	(Look in paragraph 3)

3 *Compare:* What was the *same* about the wise man and foolish man? Write your answer on the lines in the box.

Day 5

Skills: Connecting Writing with Reading

1 Read the story as an *independent reader* to someone in your home. Ask for help if you get stuck on a word. You are a wonderful reader!

2 On the lines below, write about the following: *We read a story about houses. Write about building a strong house. What do you think a strong house needs?*

Use the guide below for writing. Sentence 1 is your topic sentence. Sentences 2–4 support your topic sentence. Sentence 5 is your concluding sentence.

Topic Sentence: Copy this sentence on the line below: *A strong house needs many things.*

_____ .

Supporting Sentence: *A strong house needs . . .*

_____ .

Supporting Sentence: *A strong house also needs . . .*

_____ .

Supporting Sentence: *Another thing a strong house needs is . . .*

_____ .

Concluding Sentence: Think of a sentence to end your paragraph!

_____ .

After you finish your sentences, read them aloud to someone in your home.

Day 6

Skills: Visualization, Sentences

Use your writing tools to *draw and color a picture*. Draw a picture of what the houses looked like after the rains, storms, and winds came. Write a sentence about each of your pictures on the lines below.

The house on a rock.	**The house on sand.**

1._____

2._____

When you are finished, read your sentences aloud to someone.

Fluency Check

Set the timer for one minute, and see how many words in the story you can read correctly. You are a Mighty Reader!

Jesus and the Storm

Vocabulary

The list of words below will be in the story. Take a few minutes to discuss the meanings of these words with your child before beginning to read. Ask your child to repeat them to you and use them in a sentence.

experienced: has knowledge about how to do something

windstorm: a storm with strong winds

rough: choppy, uneven

stern: the back part of a boat

cushion: a soft pad

terrified: extremely afraid

Biblical terms: **Jesus, disciples**

Skills

Refer to the Reading Skills Guide on page 7 for a detailed explanation about many of these skills.

Key Details

Understanding Words and Phrases

Context Clues

Inferencing

Word Analysis

Connecting Writing with Reading

Main Topic

Visualization

Text Features

Vocabulary

Jesus and the Storm

Mark 4:35–41

1 **Jesus** had been busy teaching all day. That evening, He told His **disciples** He wanted to take a trip. Jesus said He wanted to sail over to the other side of the sea. So He and His disciples left the crowd and sailed away.

2 The disciples were fishermen. They had sailed a boat many times before. They were **experienced** sailors and were not worried about the trip. So Jesus decided to take a nap.

3 Storm clouds began to roll over the boat. Soon the sky turned dark, and heavy rain began to fall. Suddenly, a powerful **windstorm** took over the sea. The **rough** waves splashed over the sides of the boat. The disciples began to feel afraid.

4 They ran to get Jesus. He was in the **stern** fast asleep. He was resting on a **cushion**. The boat was filling up with water. The disciples thought they might drown! They woke Jesus up.

5 Jesus stood and said to the storm, "Silence! Be still!" The wind and rain stopped. The sea was calm again. He turned to the disciples. Jesus asked them why they were afraid. He said, "Do you still have no faith?"

6 The disciples were **terrified** but amazed at the same time. They spoke with one another. They saw that even the wind and the sea obeyed Jesus! The disciples knew in that moment that Jesus was very powerful. He is still powerful today.

Always trust in Jesus' power, Mighty Reader!

89

Day 1

1. Read the story as an *echo read* with someone in your home.

2. Who are the *main characters* in the story? Write your answers in the boxes.

3. What is the *setting* of this story? Write your answer in the box.

4. What is the *problem* in the story? Write your answer in the box.

5. What is the *solution* to the story? Write your answer in the box.

Day 2

Skills: Understanding Words and Phrases

1 Read the story as a *choral read* with someone in your home.

2 Reread paragraph 2. What do you think the word experienced means in the following sentence? *They were experienced sailors.* Write your answer in the box.

```
┌─────────────────────────────────────────────────────────────┐
│                                                             │
│                                                             │
│                                                             │
│                                                             │
│                                                             │
└─────────────────────────────────────────────────────────────┘
```

3 Reread paragraph 3. What do you think the bold phrase means in the following sentence? *Storm clouds began to **roll over the boat**.* Write your answer in the box.

```
┌─────────────────────────────────────────────────────────────┐
│                                                             │
│                                                             │
│                                                             │
│                                                             │
│                                                             │
└─────────────────────────────────────────────────────────────┘
```

4 Reread paragraph 6. What does the following sentence tell you about Jesus' power: ***Even the wind and the sea obeyed Jesus!*** Write your answer in the box.

```
┌─────────────────────────────────────────────────────────────┐
│                                                             │
│                                                             │
│                                                             │
│                                                             │
└─────────────────────────────────────────────────────────────┘
```

Day 3

Skills: Context Clues, Inferencing

1 Read the story as a *cloze read* with someone in your home.

2 Reread paragraph 3. In the text, circle the word **rough** in (orange). What do you think the word **rough** means?

3 Look at paragraph 3 again. What kind of weather is going to happen based on the following sentences?

Storm clouds began to roll over the boat. Soon the sky turned dark.

4 In the text, circle the word **cushion** in (yellow). What do you think the word **cushion** means? Write your answer in the box.

Day 4

Skills: Word Analysis

1 Read the story as a *partner read* with someone in your home.

2 Reread paragraph 3. In the text, circle the word **windstorm** in (red). This is a *compound* word. What two words make up the word **windstorm**? Write your answer in the boxes.

3 Reread paragraph 6. In the text, circle the word **terrified** in (orange). Write the word **terrified** in the box. Trace the *vowels* in orange and the *consonants* in yellow.

4 Find the word **cushion** in paragraph 4. What is a *synonym*, a word that means the same thing, for **cushion**? Write your answer in the box.

Day 5

Skill: Connecting Writing with Reading, Main Topic

1 Read the story as an *independent reader* to someone in your home. Ask for help if you get stuck on a word. You can do it!

2 On the lines below, write about the following: Tell about the main topic of this paragraph by using key details from the story. (Look in paragraph 5 to find your key details.)

Use the guide below for writing. Sentence 1 is your topic sentence. Sentences 2-4 support your topic sentence. Sentence 5 is your concluding sentence.

Topic Sentence: Copy this sentence on the line below: *Jesus calms the storm.*

_____ .

Supporting Sentence: What did Jesus say to the storm?

_____ .

Supporting Sentence: What happened to the wind and rain?

_____ .

Supporting Sentence: What happened to the sea?

_____ .

Concluding Sentence: Think of a sentence to end your paragraph!

_____ .

After you finish your sentences, read them aloud to someone in your home.

Day 6

Skills: Visualization, Text Features

Use your writing tools to *draw and color a picture*. Draw a picture of Jesus on the boat calming the storm. *Label* different parts of your picture with words such as *Jesus, boat, sail, waves, wind, clouds,* and *dark sky*. Practice reading your labels to someone.

Fluency Check

Set the timer for one minute, and see how many words in the story you can read correctly. You are a Mighty Reader!

Jesus the Healer

Vocabulary

The list of words below will be in the story. Take a few minutes to discuss the meanings of these words with your child before beginning to read. Ask your child to repeat them to you and use them in a sentence.

begged: desperately asked for something

heal: make better

instantly: happening immediately

trembled: shook

trouble: to bother someone

rose up: stood up

Biblical terms: Jesus, Jairus

Skills

Refer to the Reading Skills Guide on page 7 for a detailed explanation about many of these skills.

Problem/Solution	Connecting Writing with Reading
Character Response	Main Idea
Key Details	Visualization
Context Clues	Compare/Contrast
Sequencing	Vocabulary
Word Analysis	

Jesus the Healer

Mark 5:21–43; Luke 8:40–56

1. A crowd of people waited for Jesus. They began to follow Him and watch His miracles. A man stepped out of the crowd. His name was Jairus. He had a daughter who was very sick.

2. When Jairus reached Jesus, he fell down to His feet. Jairus begged Jesus to come to his house. He told Jesus his twelve-year-old daughter was dying. He hoped that Jesus could heal her.

3. As Jesus walked with Jairus, He felt power leave his body. A sick woman in the crowd had touched the end of His robe. She was instantly healed. Jesus asked the crowd who had touched Him. The woman trembled at His feet. She told everyone why she had touched Jesus. Jesus said, "Your faith has healed you. Go in peace."

4. After Jesus healed the woman, some people told Jairus that his daughter had died. The people said not to trouble the teacher anymore. Jesus told Jairus not to be afraid. Jesus said, "Only believe, and she will be healed."

5. Jesus went inside Jairus's house with Peter, John, and James. Her parents were crying. Jesus said, "Stop crying because she is not dead but asleep." Then, Jesus took the girl by the hand. He told her to get up. She was alive again, and she rose up! Jesus told the girl's parents to give her something to eat.

6. Jairus and his wife were amazed at Jesus' miracle! They were thankful that their daughter was alive! Jesus healed the woman and the girl. He still heals people today.

Jesus can heal you too, Mighty Reader!

Day 1

1. Read the story as an *echo read* with someone in your home.

2. Reread paragraph 1. What was the first problem in this story? Underline evidence in yellow. Write your answer in the box.

```



```

3. Reread paragraph 2. How did Jairus respond to the problem? Underline evidence in orange. Write your answer in the box.

```



```

4. Reread paragraph 5. How did Jesus respond to the girl's parents? Underline evidence in green. Write your answer in the box.

```



```

5. How did Jesus solve the problem in paragraph 5? Underline evidence in blue. Write your answer in the box.

```



```

Day 2

Skills: Key Details

1 Read the story as a *choral read* with someone in your home.

2 Look back in the story to answer the key detail questions. Write your answers in the boxes below.

Who has a sick daughter?	
What does the sick woman touch?	
Why is Jesus late in getting to Jairus's house?	
Where does Jesus go to heal the sick girl?	
Why does Jesus tell the parents to stop crying?	
When does Jesus tell the girl to eat?	

Day 3

Skills: Context Clues, Sequencing

1. Read the story as a *cloze read* with someone in your home.

2. In the text, circle the word **heal** in (purple). What do you think the word **heal** means?

[blank response box]

3. *Sequence* the key details below by numbering the events in order as they appear in the story.

	A sick woman in the crowd touched the end of Jesus' robe.
	Jesus went inside Jairus's house.
	Jairus begged Jesus to come to his house.
	Jesus took the girl by the hand and told her to get up.

4. Reread this sentence: *The people said not to trouble the teacher anymore.* What does the word **trouble** mean in the sentence? Choose an answer below.

O To solve a problem
O To get caught making a bad choice
O To bother someone

Day 4

Skills: Word Analysis

1   Read the story as a *partner read* with someone in your home.

2   Write *synonyms* for the following vocabulary words below. A *synonym* is a word that means almost the same thing as another word.

trembled	
rose up	

3   Write *rhyming* words for the vocabulary words below. A *rhyming* word is a word that has the same ending sound as another word.

heal	
trouble	

4   Reread this sentence: *She was instantly healed.* The word **instantly** means it happened right away. Write the word **instantly** in the box below. Trace the *vowels* in orange and the *consonants* in yellow.

Day 5

Skills: Connecting Writing with Reading, Main Idea

1 Read the story as an *independent reader* to someone in your home. Ask for help if you get stuck on a word. Keep practicing, and you will become a stronger reader!

2 On the lines below, write about the main idea of Jesus as a healer.

Use the guide below for writing. Sentence 1 is your topic sentence. Sentences 2–3 support your topic sentence. Sentence 4 is your concluding sentence.

Topic Sentence: Copy this sentence on the line below: *Jesus was a great healer.*

_____ .

Supporting Sentence: *Jesus healed . . .*

_____ .

Supporting Sentence: *Jesus also healed . . .*

_____ .

Concluding Sentence: Think of a sentence to end your paragraph!

_____ .

After you finish your sentences, read them aloud to someone in your home.

Day 6

Skills: Visualization, Compare/Contrast

Use your writing tools to *draw and color a picture*. Let's illustrate to *compare and contrast* how Jairus and his wife felt when their daughter was sick and how they felt when she was healed. Use your mind to *visualize* how their faces might have looked during each situation. Draw a picture to answer each of the questions.

How did the parents feel when their daughter was sick?	How did the parents feel when their daughter was healed?

Fluency Check

Set the timer for one minute, and see how many words in the story you can read correctly. You are a Mighty Reader!

The Good Samaritan

Vocabulary

The list of words below will be in the story. Take a few minutes to discuss the meanings of these words with your child before beginning to read. Ask your child to repeat them to you and use them in a sentence.

neighbor: a person who lives around us and in our lives

attacked: harmed someone physically

travelers: people who are on a trip from one place to another

compassion: concern for others

inn: a place to pay and sleep for the night, a hotel

repaid: gave someone money that was owed

mercy: grace; not receiving the bad results we deserve

Biblical terms: **Jesus, priest, Levite, Good Samaritan**

Skills

Refer to the Reading Skills Guide on page 7 for a detailed explanation about many of these skills.

Sequencing Events	Inferencing
Key Details	Connecting Writing with Reading
Context Clues	Determining the Lesson
Homophones	Making Connections
Visualization	Vocabulary

The Good Samaritan

Luke 10:25–37

1. **Jesus** told parables to teach lessons to His followers. One parable He told was about a **Good Samaritan**. It was a story about loving your **neighbor** as yourself. This story explained Jesus' words.

2. In the story, a man was traveling on a road between two cities. Then some robbers **attacked** him. They beat him up badly. Then they ran away and left him to die.

3. There were other **travelers** that day too. First, a **priest** passed by. He saw the hurt man but continued on his way. Second, a **Levite** walked by. He did not help the hurt man either. Third, a Samaritan walked up to the hurt man. The Samaritan had **compassion**.

4. The Samaritan helped the man. He bandaged the man's wounds. Then he placed the hurt man on his own animal. He took the hurt man to an **inn**. He also paid the innkeeper to take care of the hurt man after he left. The Samaritan said he would **repay** any more money that was spent to take care of the man.

5. Jesus asked the people which of the three men was a good neighbor. It was the man who showed **mercy**. Jesus said all the people should go and do the same.

6. We are to love our neighbor as ourselves. We should treat others as we would want to be treated. We should be like the Good Samaritan.

Remember to show mercy to others, Mighty Reader!

Day 1

Skills: Sequencing Events, Key Details

1. Read the story as an *echo read* with someone in your home.

2. Reread paragraph 3. Circle the three *sequencing* words in (yellow).

3. *Sequence* the events from paragraph 3 and fill in the chart below.

Sequencing Word	Who was the traveler?	What did the traveler do?

4. Reread paragraph 1. Why did Jesus use parables? Write your answer in the box.

Day 2

Skills: Context Clues, Key Details

1 Read the story as a *choral read* with someone in your home.

2 Reread paragraph 2. What is the *setting* of the story? Write your answer in the box.

3 (Circle) the word **repay** in the text. What do you think this word means? Write it in box 1. What is the root word in **repay**? Write it in box 2.

1.
2.

4 There are a lot of characters in this story. Who do you think is the *main character*? In the text, circle what he is called in (yellow). Write your answer in the box.

Day 3

Skills: Homophones, Visualization, Context Clues

1 Read the story as a *cloze read* with someone in your home.

2 Reread paragraphs 2 and 4. In the text, use (orange) to circle the word **road** in paragraph 2 and **inn** in paragraph 4. These are examples of *homophones*. They are words that sound the same as other words but are spelled differently and have different meanings. After reading, draw a picture to represent the meanings of each of these words in the story.

Road	Inn

3 What does the word **attacked** mean in paragraph 2?

O Called someone a name
O Brought harm to a person's body
O Helped someone in need

Day 4

Skills: Key Details, Inferencing

1 Read the story as a *partner read* with someone in your home.

2 Reread paragraph 4. Find three ways the Samaritan helped the hurt man. Write your answers in the boxes.

1.
2.
3.

3 How do you think the hurt man felt after he realized the Samaritan had taken care of him? Write your answer in the box.

4 What do you think it means to be a Good Samaritan? Write your answer in the box.

Day 5

Skills: Connecting Writing with Reading,
Determining the Lesson

1 Read the story as an *independent reader* to someone in your home. Ask for help if you get stuck on a word. You're a great reader!

2 On the lines below, write about the following: *This parable teaches us to show compassion to others. How did the Samaritan show compassion to the hurt man?*

Use the guide below for writing. Sentence 1 is your topic sentence. Sentences 2–4 support your topic sentence. Sentence 5 is your concluding sentence.

Topic Sentence: Copy this sentence on the line: *The Samaritan showed compassion to the man.*

_____.

Supporting Sentence: How did the Samaritan help the hurt man with his wounds?

_____.

Supporting Sentence: How did he help the hurt man get to the inn?

_____.

Supporting Sentence: How did he help the hurt man at the inn?

_____.

Concluding Sentence: Think of a sentence to end your paragraph!

_____.

After you finish your sentences, read them aloud to someone in your home.

Day 6

Skills: Visualization, Making Connections

Reread paragraph 5. Jesus tells us to the do the same as the Good Samaritan. Use your writing tools to *draw and color a picture* of yourself helping someone in need. Some examples would be helping your mom carry in the groceries or helping your dad with the yard work.

Write a sentence about your picture in the box below. Explain how you are being a Good Samaritan. Share your sentence with someone.

Fluency Check

Set the timer for one minute, and see how many words in the story you can read correctly. You are a Mighty Reader!

Read:

"For I know the plans I have for you"—this is the Lord's declaration—"plans for your well-being, not for disaster, to give you a future and a hope."
—Jeremiah 29:11

Remember:

As you read the Bible, you will hear more and more stories about how God took care of His people. He gave them homes, families, and protection. If you believe in Jesus, then you belong to God's people too! Jeremiah 29:11 says that God has a plan to give you hope and a future. He will always be with you, Mighty Reader. Remember this fact as you read Bible stories. Look for ways God helps the people He loves, even when things get hard. He is an all-knowing and all-powerful God, and He has great plans for you!

Think:

1. Which Bible story in this workbook was your favorite? Why? What can you learn from it?

2. Think about Joshua from the story "Joshua and the Walls." What were God's plans for him? How did God provide Joshua a hope and a future?

3. Think about Jesus' miracles you read about in this book. Does that give you hope that Jesus has power to do great things for you too?

4. What do you want to be when you grow up, Mighty Reader?

5. As you grow, you will begin to have more hopes for your future. What is something exciting you hope to do? Do you think it is in God's plans for you?

6. Ask God to help you make good decisions as you grow. What will you share with Him in your prayers today?

God has plans for you, Mighty Reader!